Teach Your Dog

JAPANESE

Rugby World Cup 2019
Travel Edition

Japanese is easy. More than 125 million people who live in Japan and their 11 million dogs use it every day. With the help of this book, your dog will soon be using Japanese every day too.

PROFESSOR IAN NEARY
ST ANTONY'S COLLEGE, OXFORD UNIVERSITY

I believe that language learning should be fun and enjoyable with good visual aids.
This book, with Anne's lovely illustrations, gives dogs and their owners a fun way of learning Japanese.

SUZUKO ANAI
AUTHOR OF 'LET'S READ JAPANESE'
BY OXFORD BROOKES UNIVERSITY

A brilliant Japanese phrase book for rugby fans – and dog lovers!

NIGEL BOTHERWAY
RUGBY WRITER,
THE SUNDAY TIMES

Teach Your Dog

JAPANESE
RUGBY WORLD CUP 2019
TRAVEL EDITION

Anne Cakebread

Thank you to:
Helen, Marcie, Frieda and Lily, my family,
friends and neighbours in St Dogmaels for all
their support and encouragement, Carolyn at
Y Lolfa and Suzuko Anai & Ian Neary for
Japanese translations and pronunciations.
Arigatō gozaimasu.

First impression 2019

© Anne Cakebread & Y Lolfa Cyf., 2019

Illustrations and design by Anne Cakebread

ISBN: 978-1-912631-12-4

Published and printed in Wales on paper from well-maintained forests by Y Lolfa Cyf., Talybont, Ceredigion, SY24 5HE Wales
e-mail ylolfa@ylolfa.com
website www.ylolfa.com
tel +44 1970 832 304
fax +44 1970 832 782

"Rugby World Cup"

"Ragubī Wārudo Kappu"

pron:

"Rag-oo-bee Wah-roo-do Ca-poo"

'o' as in 'hot'

pause slightly after this syllable

"Hello"

"Konnichiwa"

pron:

"<u>Kon</u>-nee-chee-w<u>a</u>"

pause
slightly
after this
syllable

'a'
as in
'm<u>a</u>n'

"My name is ..."

"Watashi-wa ... desu"

pron:
"Wa-tash-ee-wa ... dess"

'a' as in 'man'

'a' as in 'man'

"Nice to meet you"

"Hajimemashite"

pron:

"Ha-jim-e-mash-it-e"

'a' as in 'man'

'e' as in 'met'

"Good morning"

"Ohayō gozaimasu"

pron:

"O-hi-yo gozz-eye-mass"

'o' as in 'hot'

'o' as in 'more'

"Good evening"

"Konbanwa"

pron:

"Con-ban-wa"

'a'
as in
'man'

"Goodnight"

"Oyasumi-nasai"

pron:

"Oi-<u>a</u>-sue-mee-n<u>a</u>ss-eye"

'a'
as in
'm<u>a</u>n'

"Where is
the stadium?"

"Sutajiamu-wa
doko desu-ka?"

pron:
"Sue-tadge-ee-yam-oo
-wa dock-o dess-ka?"

'a'
as in
'man'

'o'
as in
'hot'

'a'
as in
'man'

"Thank you"

"Arigatō gozaimasu"

'a' as in 'm<u>a</u>n'

'o' as in 'm<u>o</u>re'

pron:

"<u>A</u>-rig-at-<u>o</u>
gozz-eye-mass"

"What a kick!"

"Sugoi kikku!"

pron:

"Sue-goy _kick_-koo!"

pause slightly after this syllable

"scrum"
"sukuramu"
pron:
"skoo-ram-oo"

"knock on"
"nokkuon"
pron:
"nock-oo-on"

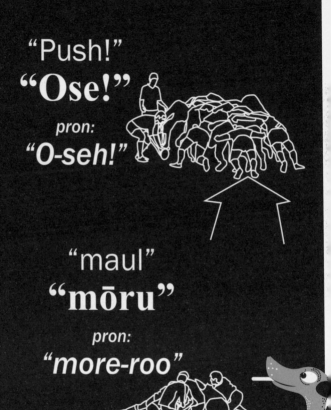

"Foul!"
"Fauru!"
pron:
"Fow-roo!"

"What a try!"
"Sugoi torai!" トヨ
pron:
"Sue-goy to-rye!"

"Tackle!"
"Takkuru!"
pron:
"Tack-oo-roo!"

"line out"
"rain auto"
pron:
"rine ow-to" as in hot

"What's the score?"

"Sukoa-wa nan-ten desu-ka?"

pron:

"Sue-k<u>oa</u>-w<u>a</u> nan-ten dess-k<u>a</u>?"

'oa'
as in
'b<u>oa</u>'

'a'
as in
'm<u>a</u>n'

'a'
as in
'm<u>a</u>n'

"pass"

"pāsu"

pron:

"pah-sue"

"full time"

"no-saido"

pron:

"noss-eye-do"

'o'
as in
'hot'

"Congratulations!"

"Omedetō!"

pron:
"O-medet-o!"

'o' as in 'hot'

'o' as in 'more'

"How are you?"

"Genki desu-ka?"

pron:

"**Ge**nky dess-k**a**?"

'Ge'
as in
'**ge**t'

'a'
as in
'm**a**n'

"I'm good/fine"

"Genki desu"

pron:

<u>Ge</u>nky dess

'Ge'
as in
'g<u>e</u>t'

"Please"

"Onegai shimasu"

pron:

"O̱-ne̱h-guy shimass"

'o'
as in
'ho̱t'

'e'
as in
'me̱t'

"See you later!"

"Mata ne!"

pron:

"Matta neh!"

'a' as in 'man'

'e' as in 'met'

"I'm sorry"

"Gomen-nasai"

pron:

"Go-men-nass-eye"

'o'
as in
'hot'

'a'
as in
'man'

"Where is the toilet?"

"Toire-wa doko desu-ka?"

'e' as in 'met'

'a' as in 'man'

pron:

"Toy-reh-wa dock-o dess-ka?"

'o' as in 'hot'

'a' as in 'man'

"Do you speak English?"

"Eigo-ga dekimasu-ka?"

pron:

"Ay-go-ga decky mass-ka?"

'Ay' as in 'say'

'o' as in 'hot'

'a' as in 'man'

"Yes"

"Hai"

pron:
"Hi"

"No"

"Īe"

pron:

"Ee-yeh"

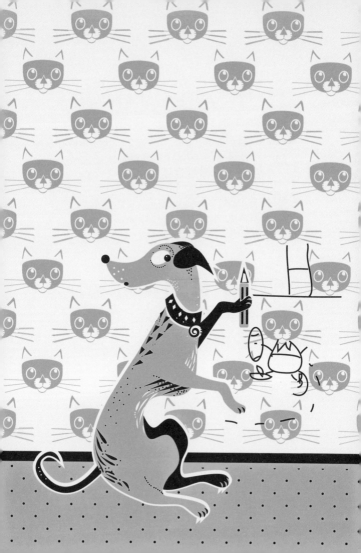

"Excuse me"

"Sumimasen"

pron:
"Sue-me-mass-en"

"Do you have an English menu?"

"Eigo-no menyū arimasu-ka?"

'Ay' as in 'say'

pron:

'o' as in 'hot'

"Ay-go-no men-yoo arimass-ka?"

'a' as in 'man'

"How much is this?"

"Ikura desu-ka?"

pron:

"I-koo-ra dess-ka?"

'I'
as in
'it'

'a'
as in
'man'

"A beer, please"

"Bīru-o kudasai"

pron:

"Bee-roo-o koo-dass-eye"

'o'
as in
'hot'

'a'
as in
'man'

"Cheers!"

"Kanpai!"

pron:
"Camp-eye!"

"Enjoy!"
(before a meal)

"Itadakimasu!"

pron:
"Itta-dacky-mass!"

'a'
as in
'man'

"It's delicious"

"Oishī desu"

pron:

"O-i-she dess"

'O'
as in
'hot'

'i'
as in
'it'

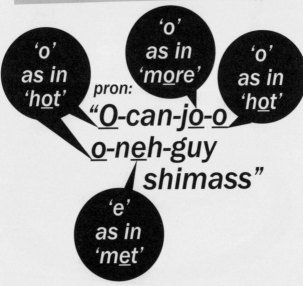

"Thank you!"
(after a meal)

"Gochisō sama deshita!"

pron:

"Gochi-saw samma deshta!"

'o' as in 'h**o**t'

'i' as in '**i**t'

1 一
"ichi"
pron:
"itchy"

2 二
"ni"
pron:
"nee"

3 三
"san"

pron:
"san"

'a'
as in
'm<u>a</u>n'

4 四
"shi"

pron:
"she"

5 五
"go"
pron:
"go"

'o' as in 'hot'

6 六
"roku"
pron:
"rock-oo"

7 七
"shichi"

pron:
"sh-itchy"

8 八
"hachi"

pron:
"hatchy"

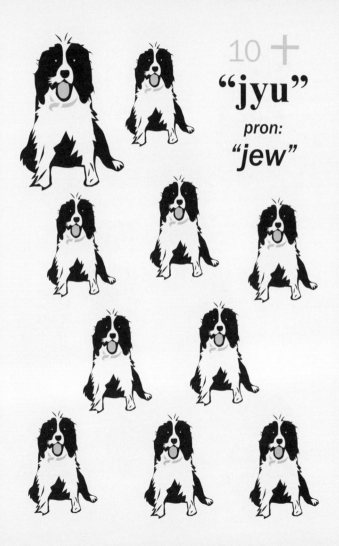

10 +

"jyu"

pron:

"jew"

"I/We want to go to..."

"**...-ni ikitai desu**"

pron:

"...-nee icky-tie dess"

"What platform?"

"**Purattofōmu-wa nan-ban desu-ka?**"

pron:

"*Poo-ratto-form-oo-wa nan-ban dess-ka?*"

'a' as in 'man'

"Which train goes to...?"

"...-iki ressha-wa dore desu-ka?"

pause slightly after this syllable

pron:

"...-icky resh-a-wa do-reh dess-ka?"

'o' as in 'hot'

'e' as in 'met'

'a' as in 'man'

"first-class carriage"

"green-sha"

pron:
"goo-reen-<u>sha</u>"

'sha'
as in
'<u>shall</u>'

"One way"

"Kata-michi"

pron:

"K<u>a</u>tt<u>a</u> mitchy"

'a'
as in
'm<u>a</u>n'

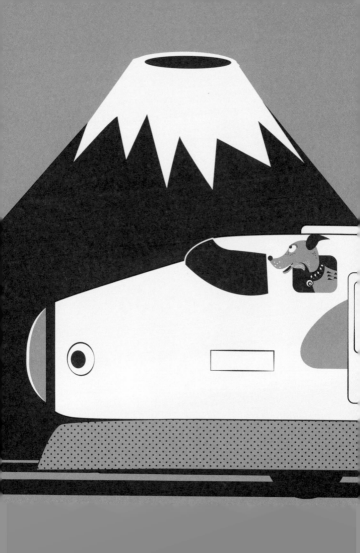

"Round-trip"/"Return"

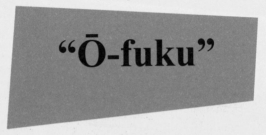

"Ō-fuku"

pron:

"O-fookoo"

'O'
as in
'more'

"Where am I right now?"

"Koko-wa doko desu-ka?"

pron:
"Cock-<u>o</u>-w<u>a</u> dock-<u>o</u> dess-k<u>a</u>?"

'a' as in 'm<u>a</u>n'

'o' as in 'h<u>o</u>t'

"Go left"

"Hidari-ni itte kudasai"

pron:

"Hidaree-nee it-e koo-dass-eye"

'e' as in 'met'

pause slightly after this syllable

"Go right"

"Migi-ni itte kudasai"

pron:

"Miggy-nee it-e koo-dass-eye"

pause slightly after this syllable

'e' as in 'met'

"Go straight on"

"Massugu itte kudasai"

pron:

"<u>Mass</u>-oo-goo <u>it</u>-e koo-dass-eye"

'e' as in 'm<u>e</u>t'

pause slightly after this syllable

"Please can you call me a taxi?"

"Takushi-o yonde kudasai?"

pron:

"Tack-oo-she-<u>o</u> yond<u>e</u>h koo-dass-eye?"

'o' as in 'h<u>o</u>t'

'e' as in 'm<u>e</u>t'

"Here, please"

"Koko de,
onegai shimasu"

pron:

"Cock-o deh,
o-neh-guy shimass"

'e' as in 'met'

'o' as in 'hot'

'o' as in 'hot'

'e' as in 'met'

"I'm from ..."

"...-kara kimashita"

pron:

"...-ca-ra kimashta"

'a'
as in
'man'

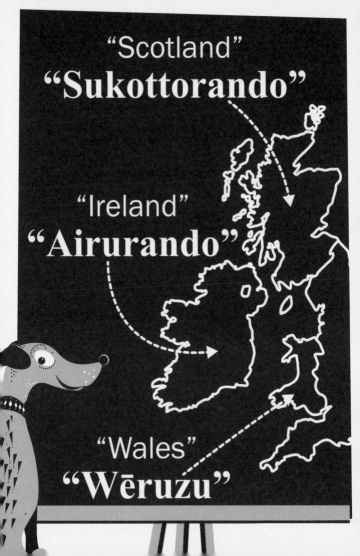

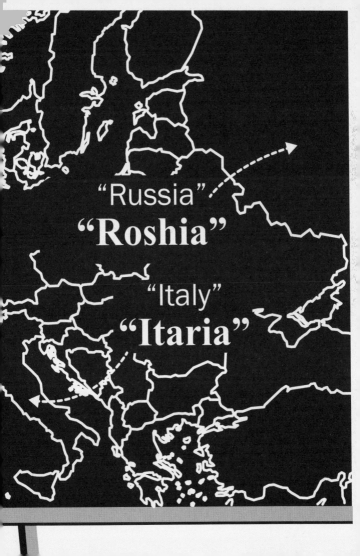

"Goodbye"

"Sayonara"

pron:

"Sigh-o-na-ra"

'o'
as in
'hot'

'a'
as in
'man'

Other titles in this series include:

Teach Your Dog Welsh
Teach Your Cat Welsh
Teach Your Dog Cornish
Teach Your Dog Māori
Teach Your Dog Irish
(Rugby World Cup 2019 Travel Edition)